CELEBRATING KWANZAA

The first step forward is a step backward to Africa and our roots.
We use the past as a foundation on which to construct our future.

Maulana Karenga

LIBRARY OF CONGRESS CATALOGING-IN-PUBLICATION DATA

Hoyt-Goldsmith, Diane.
    Celebrating Kwanzaa / by Diane Hoyt-Goldsmith : photographs by
Lawrence Migdale. — 1st ed.
        p.   cm.
    Includes index.
    Summary: Text and photographs depict how a Chicago family
celebrates the African American holiday, Kwanzaa.
    ISBN 0-8234-1048-X
    1. Kwanzaa — Juvenile literature.   [1. Kwanzaa, 2. Afro
-Americans — Social life and customs.]   I. Migdale, Lawrence, ill.
II. Title.
GT4403.H69   1993   93-16799
394.2'68 — dc20   CIP
ISBN 0-8234-1130-3 (pbk.)   AC

The NGUZO SABA on p. 8 is used by permission of the University of Sankore Press,
Los Angeles from *The African American Holiday of Kwanzaa: A Celebration of Family,
Community, and Culture* by Maulana Karenga, 1988.

ACKNOWLEDGMENTS

In creating this book, we enjoyed the cooperation and enthusiasm of many people. We wish to thank the Barnes family — Mike and Mari, Max and Andiey — for sharing this very special holiday with us. Their warm hospitality and friendship made our visit with them unforgettable. We would also like to thank the rest of their family and friends who came to share the Kwanzaa Karamu: Grandma, Fan, Ruth, Mama Charlotte, Aunt Charlotte, Ann, Bonnie Kelly, Brandi and Mario, Aunt Shirley, Evelyn, Linda and Jason; and Gary, Chris, and their mom.

    We greatly appreciate the time we were able to spend with Maulana and Tiamoyo Karenga. Our conversations about Kwanzaa greatly enriched our understanding of the principles that provide the foundation for this celebration. The staff of the African American Cultural Center in Los Angeles was also very helpful.

    We would like to thank all the other people who helped to make the project a success: Katrina Carter; Gloria Burns of Gloria's Glamour Girl Salon; C.J. Appleson Smith and the staff of the Kohl Children's Museum in Wilmette, IL; Shanta, an African American storyteller; Joyce Ann Clark of Rainbo-Rink; Baba Tyehimba Mtu, drummer; Edward J. Hall, airbrush artist; and the wonderful couple from Ghana whose names have been lost but whose generosity is not forgotten. We would also like to thank dance teacher Jeri Williams and the girls in the Bedia Bure Dance Group of the Boulevard Arts Center in Chicago for the wonderful performance they shared with us, and the people at the Chicago Cultural Center for their cooperation. Finally, we would like to thank Kimberly, Margaret, and Tiffany of the Commonwealth Community Church Choir and their director, Anna, for participating in this project.

    We give special thanks to Pat Redd, who helped in the early stages of our research, and Lorna Mason who gave a historian's perspective on the manuscript.

CELEBRATING KWANZAA

BY DIANE HOYT-GOLDSMITH

PHOTOGRAPHS BY LAWRENCE MIGDALE

HOLIDAY HOUSE • NEW YORK

In the spirit of Kwanzaa,
we dedicate this book to
Maulana and Tiamoyo Karenga,
to the "master teacher" and "she who inspires"—
and to
Terry Lowenthal and David Goldsmith,
our inspiration and greatest support.

Andiey is in the eighth grade. The watch she is wearing was a prize she won at school for scoring high on a reading test.

My name is Andria Ruth Barnes, but everyone just calls me Andiey (AN-dee). I am thirteen years old, and I live in Chicago, Illinois, with my mother and father and my little brother. His name is Michael Paxton Barnes, but we call him Max, a nickname that is as small as he is.

On the first day of Kwanzaa, Andiey and Max walk home from the store through their Chicago neighborhood. It is cold — the temperature is only 20 degrees.

Max is five years old and goes to kindergarten. The hat he is wearing is called a kufi (koo-fee).

In the winter, Chicago can be a hard city to live in. Everyone in my family hates cold weather, especially my mother. She has lived here all her life, and yet each year, when the temperature drops and the snow begins to fall, she wonders why we haven't moved to a warmer place.

Winter is the time when we celebrate Kwanzaa (KWAN-zah), the African American festival of the harvest. Kwanzaa begins the day after Christmas and lasts for seven days. It is a time to reflect upon the year that is ending and to celebrate our African heritage.

The word Kwanzaa comes from a Kiswahili (kee-swah-HEE-lee) phrase that means "first fruits." Kiswahili is a language that is understood by people in many parts of Africa. The holiday was patterned after harvest festivals that still take place in Africa at the end of the Old Year and the beginning of the New Year.

Kwanzaa is not a religious holiday. Instead, it's an expression of pride in our African American heritage. It is a holiday celebrated by people of many different religious beliefs.

Kwanzaa is spelled with seven letters, and it takes place over seven days and nights. There are seven symbols for the holiday. But most important, there are seven principles or values that are celebrated during Kwanzaa, one for each day of the week. These are called the Nguzo Saba (en-GOO-zoh SAH-bah).

HOW KWANZAA STARTED

Kwanzaa was created in 1966 by an African American named Maulana Karenga (Mah-oo-LAN-nah Kar-REN-gah). In a great act of Kuumba or creativity, he designed a holiday that is now celebrated by more than eighteen million people in the United States. He developed a way to restore African cultural traditions to the African American people.

When our African ancestors were brought here as slaves in the early days of the colonies, often they were forced to give up their name, their language, their religion, and their culture. Many were cut off from their roots and their history. In the 1960s, as part of the civil rights movement, black people began to rediscover their rich cultural heritage by looking back to Africa for inspiration.

At this time, many blacks began to choose African names. Karenga's first name, Maulana, means "master teacher" in Kiswahili. This name was given to him by the people he worked with because of his talents as a teacher.

Fashions like dashikis (dah-SHEE-kees) and clothing made from kente (KEN-tay) cloth woven in Africa became popular with African Americans. They wore their hair naturally in Afro styles. Tiny braids called "cornrows" became popular, too. People all over the United States began to learn and use African languages like Kiswahili.

Colleges and universities developed black studies programs that focused on the thoughts, experiences, and history of Africans and African Americans. Communities built new theaters where plays were performed by and about black people, as well as dance programs and music. Museums with an emphasis on black culture and history were started.

Maulana Karenga, and others like him, traveled to Africa to visit countries like Senegal, Nigeria, and Egypt to learn firsthand about the traditions and values of the African people. Karenga feels that the family and community values that have existed throughout history in Africa can be brought to the United States to enrich black culture. He created the Nguzo Saba, the list of the seven Kwanzaa principles, to teach these values to other African Americans.

Maulana Karenga studied about harvest festivals in Africa to get ideas for the celebration of Kwanzaa in the United States. He holds two doctorate degrees and has devoted his life to a career as an educator and community leader.

THE SYMBOLS OF KWANZAA

The kinara is the centerpiece for the celebration of Kwanzaa. Surrounding it are the other Kwanzaa symbols, arranged on the handmade mkeka.

As people prepare for the celebration of Kwanzaa, they gather seven important symbols to display in their homes during the holiday. The words *mazao, mkeka, kikombe cha umoja, kinara, mishumaa saba, muhindi,* and *zawadi* are Kiswahili terms for these symbols.

MAZAO (mah-ZAH-oh) are the fruits and vegetables of the harvest. As in the early days of African history, farmers still work together to raise crops for food. The harvest is a time of joy and thanksgiving. Having a bountiful harvest shows that the farmers have cooperated and are successful. The mazao, the fruits of the harvest, stand for the origins of Kwanzaa.

MKEKA (em-KAY-kah) is the mat on which all the other symbols rest. Often it is woven out of grasses. Some people use mats made in Africa, but many others weave their own out of fabric or strips of paper. The mkeka is a symbol of tradition and history.

KIKOMBE CHA UMOJA (kee-KOM-bay CHA oo-MOH-jah) is the unity cup. It is used to pour a libation (ly-BAY-shun), called "tambiko" (tam-BEE-koh), in honor of the ancestors. These ancestors are all the people who have come before us, including such great African Americans as Harriet Tubman and Martin Luther King, Jr. They are also the enslaved Africans who struggled to survive, to raise their families, and to build a new life of freedom. When people drink from the simple wooden cup, they honor all the people who lived before them. The cup is a symbol of unity.

KINARA (kee-NAH-rah) is the candle holder with places for seven candles. It should be simple and is often handmade. The kinara is a symbol for the African people who are the ancestors of African Americans.

MISHUMAA SABA (mee-shu-MAH SAH-bah) are the seven candles of Kwanzaa. They represent the seven principles, the Nguzo Saba. There is one black candle, three red candles, and three green ones. On each night of Kwanzaa, a new candle is lit until on the last day, they are all kindled together. The black candle is in the center, with red candles to the left and green candles to the right.

Andiey weaves together pieces of black, red, and green construction paper to make the mkeka, the mat, for her family's Kwanzaa celebration.

MUHINDI (moo-HIN-dee) are ears of dry corn, one for each child living in the household. Some people have an extra ear of corn to symbolize unborn generations. The ears of corn are the "fruit" of the cornstalk. The ears represent the dream of parents that their own children and future generations will grow strong.

ZAWADI (zah-WAH-dee) are the Kwanzaa gifts that parents give to their children. By having lived according to the Kwanzaa values during the year, the children can now "reap" the harvest of their work. Parents like to give educational games and books, or special handmade gifts. In this way, even the zawadi can help reinforce the values of Kwanzaa.

UMOJA

(oo-MOH-jah)

Unity

*Umoja means unity
for our family and community.*
— *Mari Barnes*

*America is not like a blanket — one piece
of unbroken cloth, the same color, the
same texture, the same size. America is
more like a quilt — many patches, many
pieces, many colors, many sizes, all
woven and held together by a common
thread. Even in our fractured state, all of
us count and all of us fit in somewhere.*

**Jesse Jackson (1941 -),
political and civil rights leader**

On the first night of Kwanzaa, we gather around the kinara and light one candle for Umoja or unity. Then we talk about what unity means to our family and community. For many people, this principle is the most important part of the entire Kwanzaa celebration. Being united makes us stronger because we can all work together.

My mother first celebrated Kwanzaa when she was fifteen years old. Because her father was tired of the commercialism of Christmas, he welcomed the new holiday with its emphasis on values rather than gifts. My mother tells me that in those days, her aunt would always light the candles. She learned that the black candle stands for the African American people, the red ones stand for the Blacks' struggle for justice, and the green ones represent hope for the future.

Most people begin by lighting the black candle on the first night of Kwanzaa. The next night they light a red candle. On the third night they light a green one, and continue to alternate back and forth until the last night, when all the candles burn together. This is done to symbolize that the struggle comes first and then the reward. To make Kwanzaa principles easy for us to understand, my mother wrote short poems about each one. When we light the candles, we recite the poem we've learned.

I am lucky to have many relatives living in Chicago. My great-great-grandmother, Mattie Harper, is ninety-eight years old. She tells us wonderful stories about the days when she was young. She was born in 1895, before the turn of the century. During her lifetime, she has seen how inventions like the airplane, automobile, telephone, and computer have changed our world. She still can't quite believe that men have walked on the moon.

We all call my great-great-grandmother "Grandma." She has three children, twelve grandchildren, more than twenty great-grandchildren, and too many great-great-grandchildren to count.

Grandma still gets out a lot. She and her daughter, Mama Charlotte, go to play bingo two or three times a week. My mother teases her about her winnings. "You earn as much as you would in a full-time job!" my mother tells her.

The principle of Umoja begins the holiday celebration — because Kwanzaa is for everyone. Young and old, we must all work together if we want to build a better world.

(page 10) In Andiey's family, the person who lights the kinara can pick which candle to light first. Max is chosen to light a candle for Umoja.

KUJICHAGULIA

(KOO-gee-CHA-goo-LEE-ah)

Self-determination

We name ourselves.
We define ourselves.
We are our own creation.
—*Mari Barnes*

When Malcolm X began to study his people's history for the first time, he dropped his last name. He learned that it came from a man who held his ancestors in slavery and whose name was Little. He took the last name X as a sign of his own self-determination.

Maulana Karenga (1941–), teacher and community leader

Andiey and her friend, Katrina, express themselves when they go roller skating.

My favorite day of Kwanzaa is the second day when we celebrate Kujichagulia. On this day we think about self-determination. This is the struggle to find out and express who we are as individuals, and who we are as African Americans.

Self-determination is important to the black people in America because our history has been clouded by a lack of freedom. In 1619, the first Africans were brought to Virginia from Africa through the Caribbean, where they had been indentured servants. In the years that followed, nearly four million black people were enslaved in the United States. These slaves and their descendants were forced to work, without freedom or pay, in a new country founded on the principle "that all men are created equal."

Their African names were taken away. Often children were separated from their parents, and husbands were sold to different owners from those of their wives. People were not allowed to speak African languages. Many of these men and women soon lost their identity and the links to their homeland. What remains of their history is recalled through stories that have been passed down from one generation to the next. The enslaved Africans created songs, called spirituals, that helped keep the past alive.

This year my brother's school has adopted the principle of Kujichagulia as a way of focusing on the importance of self-determination. Instead of room numbers, each classroom has been named for an African American hero. Max studies in a classroom named after Harold Washington, one of Chicago's mayors and a leader in the black community. When the students go to school, they see the names of great African American men and women everyday.

Self-determination means we have the freedom to make our own decisions. We have the power to make changes. Together we can create and build the kind of world that we want to live in.

Andiey spends some money she received as a Christmas present to have a T-shirt airbrushed with her name. The painter, who was once a graffiti artist, has his own business. He uses his talents to design a special shirt for each customer.

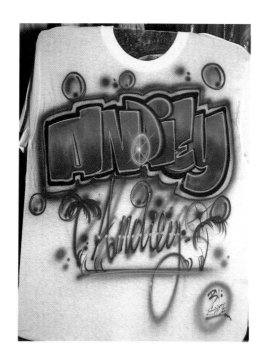

UJIMA

(oo-GEE-mah)

Collective Work and Responsibility

Working together for others, we are the keepers of our sisters and brothers.
– Mari Barnes

I cannot sit idly by in Atlanta and not be concerned about what happens in Birmingham. Injustice anywhere is a threat to justice everywhere.... Whatever affects one directly, affects all indirectly.
Martin Luther King, Jr. (1929 - 1968), minister and civil rights leader

On the third night of Kwanzaa, we light a candle for Ujima, which means collective work and responsibility. We do this because we think it is important to help each other by working together.

Both of my parents have jobs. My father works for the U.S. Postal Service. He goes to work early each morning and gets back at four in the afternoon, just as my brother and I come home from school.

During the day, my mother leaves for college right after we go to school. She is studying biology and wants to have a career in the medical profession when she graduates.

Later in the afternoon, when my dad gets home, my mother leaves for her job. She works late each night as a proofreader for a large printing company. She looks for errors in spelling, punctuation, and grammar that need to be corrected before the text can be printed. Both our parents work hard to support our family.

Andiey's father drives a forklift loaded with hundreds of empty mail sacks. The sacks carried mail to the United States from other parts of the world. They have been bundled together for shipment back to the foreign post offices.

Working at a proofreader's stand, Andiey's mother checks for errors.

Andiey helps out by washing the dishes while her mother is at work.

Max and I help out around the house. I wash the dishes, clean the floors, and look after my little brother. He does a few chores, too. These are ways Max and I can help our family.

Each spring we plant a small patch of vegetables in our backyard. This is one of Max's favorite jobs. But last spring, Max couldn't wait for my mother to come home before he started to plant the garden. He took a packet of seeds for mustard greens and scattered them everywhere. All summer long we had mustard greens coming up between the tomatoes, the cabbages, the green beans, and all mixed up with the collard greens. We still laugh about how Max helped!

On Kwanzaa, we think about our own family, and also about the other families in our community. We reach out to help others in need. My mother and I walked for miles in Chicago's "Walk for the Homeless." Twice a year we participate in a clothing drive for the homeless, and we help collect food donations for the poor, at school and in our church.

Even the way we talk to each other shows our concern. We call a person "brother" or "sister," even if we do not know him or her well. We all feel connected, like part of one huge family.

UJAMAA

(oo-jah-MAH)

Cooperative Economics

*Cooperative economics
is for our benefit.
Working together, we all profit.*

– Mari Barnes

The core of the civil rights problem is the matter of achieving equal opportunity in the labor market. For it stands to reason that all our other civil rights depend on that one for fulfillment. We cannot afford better education, better housing, or medical care unless we have jobs.

Whitney Young, Jr., (1921 – 1971), civil rights leader

Andiey has been coming to Gloria's Beauty Salon since she was a little girl. Gloria owns her own business and has a lot of customers.

How we spend money is the focus of the candlelighting on the fourth night of Kwanzaa. We think about the store owners, the doctors, the teachers, and the other professionals who are African Americans. The principle of Ujamaa reminds us to support them by using their services and buying their products. This is a way we can help strengthen our community.

This year there is a new program at Max's school. The students who sell candy to raise money for the school order it from black-owned businesses. This is another way that the principle of Ujamaa works in everyday life.

On the fourth night of Kwanzaa, we talk about the importance of being self-reliant. We need to depend on our own resources in order to become strong. Then we must share our success and good fortune with others to make our community stronger, too.

Each year my family visits the Ujamaa Market held on the fourth night of Kwanzaa. Here we can find everything from books to buttons, special African foods and clothing, artwork, and jewelry. There are performances by dancers, singers, and drummers of every description. It is an exciting evening.

(Bottom Left) Andiey lights the candles on the fourth night of Kwanzaa for Ujamaa. Then she explains "cooperative economics" to Max.

CHICAGO'S UJAMAA MARKET

The Ujamaa Market is set up indoors in a large hall. Colorful flags of the African nations hang from the ceiling. At one end of the room, there is a stage where drummers, dancers, and musicians perform during the evening. Everywhere there are wonderful things to buy.

My father loves to take us to the Ujamaa Market. He enjoys the challenge of bargaining with the salespeople. He takes special pride in his ability to make a good deal.

Some of the merchants who have booths at the market come from Africa. There are also African Americans who sell goods that they have brought back from the continent. Many other people have worked all year long creating handmade treasures to sell at the Ujamaa Market. It is a good place to shop for Kwanzaa zawadi. I can always find something special.

Max tries on a new shirt for Kwanzaa at the Ujamaa Market. Called a "dashiki," it was made by a woman from Ghana.

18

NIA

(NEE-ah)

Purpose

We all must believe we have great goals to achieve.
— *Mari Barnes*

I had crossed the line of which I had so long been dreaming. I was free. But there was no one to welcome me to the land of freedom. I was a stranger in a strange land, and my home after all was down in the old cabin quarter, with the old folks, and my brothers and sisters. But to this solemn resolution I came; I was free and they should be free also. I would make a home for them in the North, and the Lord helping me, I would bring them all here.

Harriet Tubman (c.1820 - 1913), abolitionist, spy, and scout

Max and Andiey make decorations in honor of Nia. While Andiey works on a poster, Max makes a picture of the bendera (ben-DER-rah), the African American flag. Like the colors of the mishumaa saba, the red stands for the struggle to achieve justice, the black is a symbol for the African American people, and the green stands for hope and the future.

We light the fifth candle for Nia, which means purpose. On this night, my parents want us to think carefully about our actions and the consequences of our actions. They teach us that there should be a reason or a purpose for everything that we do. They want us to believe that what we do can make a difference.

My mother says: "If you were walking home from the store and found a little boy crying because he lost his bus fare and couldn't get home, what would you do?" I answer that if I had enough money, I would give the fare to him. Then we talk about all the things that would happen because I helped the little boy. He would stop crying. He wouldn't be afraid anymore. His mother would be happy that he got home safely. Doing one small thing that is helpful makes a big difference sometimes.

As we learn more about our African roots, we realize that we come from a rich heritage that has contributed much that is good in the world. "Our heritage is better than gold," my mother says, "and we must preserve it." Because our ancestors did so much that is important, we must continue their work.

There are many ways for us to learn about our heritage. One way is through books. My mother reads to us all the time. She reads about African American leaders like Sojourner Truth, Frederick Douglass, and Shirley Chisholm. We learn about heroes who did great things for our people because they had a strong sense of purpose. She recites poems to us and reads aloud wonderful stories by African American writers.

We also learn about our heritage from exhibits at the museums in Chicago. At the Field Museum, we can see the art and objects made by African people long ago. Max and I especially like to look at the mummies and hieroglyphics from the great culture of ancient Eygpt.

We visit the Du Sable Museum of African American History, where there are changing exhibits about our culture. The museum is named after a black frontiersman and trapper, Jean Baptist Point du Sable. In 1779, du Sable built a trading post at the mouth of the Chicago River. It was the first permanent settlement in the area and made du Sable Chicago's founder.

We also learn about our heritage by listening to story-tellers. The enslaved Africans who came to America brought the storytelling tradition with them, and it has survived until today. Talking to the older people in our families and communities is another way to learn. They are often the best storytellers, with memories collected over a lifetime. They enjoy sharing these with children because it is a way for them to keep our cultural legacy alive.

Max and his mother enjoy reading a book together. Max knows how to read, but he likes to listen to stories about Africa, also.

KUUMBA

(koo-OOM-bah)

Creativity

We are charged with the duty to keep the world filled with wonder and beauty.

– Mari Barnes

Although separated from our languages, our families and customs, we had dared to live.... Through centuries of despair and dislocation, we had been creative, because we faced death by daring to hope.

Maya Angelou (1928 -), poet and writer

Max and Andiey visit the Kohl Children's Museum during Kwanzaa to hear Shanta tell stories from Africa.

On the sixth night of Kwanzaa, we celebrate Kuumba or creativity. We light a candle for all the wonderful ways in which our people have expressed themselves. African Americans have made creative contributions to our culture on every level: music and art; theater, dance, and storytelling; scholarship and politics; technology and science; exploration and sports; philosophy and religion.

Every day during Kwanzaa, we try to do things ourselves in a new way. When we needed a kinara to hold our Kwanzaa candles, my mother's cousin made one by hand, cutting it out of a single piece of wood. I love the simple, solid shape of it.

Some people are creative in the way that they dress during Kwanzaa; women wrap their heads in long pieces of colorful fabric and men wear hats called "kufis" and long tunics. Although most of us have never been to Africa, we show our appreciation of our heritage by wearing African styles.

My mother encourages us to write our own stories. When I give Max a few sheets of notebook paper, a pencil, and a little stapler, he gets busy. He works at the kitchen table, writing and drawing a story from his imagination. Before long, he has stapled together his own handmade book.

Today many black people are writing books and making movies that tell our story to the world. Some young people are learning the steps of ancient African dances and then using them to express the joy they feel today. Creating melody and rhythm, musicians and performers express the pride they feel in their culture.

On Kwanzaa, young African Americans perform a traditional basket dance that comes from South Africa. African instruments, like the drums below, are played to accompany the dancers.

The dance teacher helps a girl wrap her head in kente cloth before the performance.

23

DAY 7

IMANI

(ee-MON-ee)

Faith

*To feed our souls,
to light the way,
faith guides us through
another day.*
— *Mari Barnes*

*Without faith, nothing is possible.
With faith, nothing is impossible.*
*Mary McLeod Bethune (1875 - 1955),
educator and civil rights leader*

Andiey joins her friends in singing a hymn at choir practice. She sings with two church choirs, and people say that her voice is as beautiful as her mother's.

On the final night of Kwanzaa, we light the last of the mishumaa saba, the seventh candle. This one is for faith.

Imani is faith, the belief we have in ourselves, in our parents, in our teachers and leaders, and in our race. African Americans have needed great faith to survive the hardships of slavery and to continue the struggle for freedom, justice, and equality. Without faith, all the other principles of Kwanzaa would be empty. We know that to succeed, we have to believe that our efforts can build a better life for all African American people.

On the last night of Kwanzaa, I like to hear about Sojourner Truth. She was a woman who let faith in God and in herself direct the course of her life. She worked to help other black people gain their freedom, and she spoke out for equality not only between black people and white people, but also between women and men. She, and our other African American ancestors, have set a brave example for us to follow.

THE KWANZAA KARAMU

Family and friends are invited to attend the Kwanzaa Karamu (kah-RAH-moo) that we always have on the last day of the holiday. Karamu is a Kiswahili word that means "feast." Everyone who comes brings food to share with the group.

In our family, the Kwanzaa Karamu coincides with the celebration of the New Year. We eat special foods that we believe will bring good luck. Following an old southern tradition, my mother prepares greens, such as mustard, kale, and collards. In addition, we eat black-eyed peas and rice, a dish called "hoppin John." Although no one is quite sure where the name comes from, some believe it is from a fellow named John who came "a hoppin'" whenever his wife took this dish off the stove. Many people from the South say you have to eat black-eyed peas on New Year's Day for luck. We always do. This has become a part of my family's Kwanzaa celebration.

As Max and his dad get ready to cook for the Kwanzaa feast, Max helps his father sort through the black-eyed peas. Max has sharp eyes and tiny fingers so it is easy for him to pick out the small pebbles that sometimes get packaged in with the beans.

(page 27, top) Family and friends gather around the kinara in the living room as the Kwanzaa Karamu begins.

(page 27, bottom) Grandma takes a sip from the unity cup to honor the family's ancestors.

(Below) Max plays an African instrument, the agogo, to begin the ceremony.

My mother baked a ham, and we decorated it with little cloves pressed into a K for Kwanzaa. My godmother Bonnie brought her famous Taffy Apple Salad, and we had corn on the cob, corn bread, fruit salad, and fried chicken. For dessert, my grandmother Ann made a banana-chocolate cake, and my grandmother Fan brought a sweet potato pie.

The Kwanzaa Karamu begins when Max comes downstairs playing an African instrument called the "agogo" (ah-GOH-goh). It is made of two pieces of bell-shaped metal attached by a handle. When Max strikes the agogo with a stick, he can play two separate notes, one high and one low.

As guests arrive for the Kwanzaa Karamu, they put their contribution to the meal on one large table.

After Max appears playing the agogo, everyone gathers around the kinara in the living room. My mother begins with a libation statement to honor our ancestors. "We drink from this cup," she says, "to honor all the people who have come before us. We thank them for teaching us and for leading us. We honor them by living our lives according to their example."

Then she passes the unity cup, the kikombe cha umoja, to the oldest member of the group. Our great-great-grandmother, Mattie Harper, takes a sip of the sparkling grape juice in honor of our ancestors. When she hands the cup back, my mother asks the youngest person in the family to drink. Max takes a sip. When Max drinks, he represents the promise of each new generation because he is the youngest.

Andiey and Max join their mother in singing the family Kwanzaa song.

Then, following a family tradition, my mother, Max, and I sing a song in an African language that my mother learned when she was a little girl. She spent a lot of time with her grandfather, and he taught it to her. Now we sing it every year during Kwanzaa. We aren't sure what language the song is written in or what the words mean, but we love it very much. "We could be calling the sheep into the circle, for all I know," my mother says with a laugh.

Then we begin to light the seven candles, the mishumaa saba. As each candle starts to burn, I say the principle it celebrates out loud. Max and I recite the poems that my mother wrote to remind us of the meanings of each principle: Umoja, Kujichagulia, Ujima, Ujamaa, Nia, Kuumba, and Imani.

When all the candles are burning, our godmother Bonnie gives a short speech about what we've learned during the year, congratulates us on how we have met our challenges, and encourages us to continue in the new year along the same path.

Then my father speaks. He thanks everyone for coming to the Karamu and for participating in the celebration of Kwanzaa in our home. My father thanks the guests for the food they brought and invites them all to eat. He gives a special word to the young "brothers" present. He reminds them of the challenges they face as they grow up to be African American men. My father wishes each of them the strength to reach his dreams and the courage to live by the Kwanzaa values.

Andiey's father wears a special kufi and scarf during Kwanzaa. These were made from a traditional African fabric called mud cloth.

When Max opens his Kwanzaa gifts, he finds an educational game.

On the last day of Kwanzaa, the New Year is beginning. Although it is freezing outdoors and a cold wind blows, Andiey and her family have warm feelings for one another. As they walk along the shores of Lake Michigan, the only thing that counts is the joy of being together.

African American families celebrate Kwanzaa in their own unique ways, although there are common principles and symbols to learn about, and certain things to be done on certain days. In the spirit of Kuumba, each family takes those symbols and principles and creates a celebration based on its own values and experiences. For each family, Kwanzaa becomes an expression and a joyful celebration of what it means to be an African American.

GLOSSARY

abolitionist: Person who believes slavery to be wrong and works to bring an end to it.

Afro: Full, natural hairstyle worn by black people.

agogo: African instrument with two different sizes of metal bells. When struck with a stick, one makes a high sound and the other makes a low sound.

Angelou, Maya: (1928–) African American poet and writer.

bendera: African American flag with three stripes of red, black, and green. The black symbolizes the African American people, the red stands for their struggle for equal rights, and the green represents the hope that follows struggle.

Bethune, Mary McLeod: (1875–1955) The fifteenth child of former slaves, she founded a college for black students in Florida, served as director of the Division of Negro Affairs during Franklin D. Roosevelt's presidency, and founded the National Council of Negro Women. She dedicated her life to improving the lives of black Americans through education.

black-eyed pea: Small, white bean with a black "eye" in the center that is a staple in southern cooking.

Chisholm, Shirley: (1924–) African American leader who in 1968 became the first black woman to serve in the U.S. Congress. She was also the first woman to run for president of the United States.

cornrows: African hairstyle created by making tiny braids in rows close to the head.

dashiki: (dah-SHEE-kee) Simple African shirt worn by both men and women and made from brightly printed cloth. Although the pattern is printed, the designs resemble traditional embroidery patterns.

Douglass, Frederick: (1817–1895) A freed slave and eloquent orator who became a leader in the antislavery movement called "abolition." His autobiography, published in 1845, tells about his life as a slave.

du Sable, Jean Baptist Point: (c.1750–1818) Black frontiersman and trapper who built a trading post at the mouth of the Chicago River in 1779 and became Chicago's founder.

graffiti: (gra-FEE-tee) Rough scribblings or drawings found on public walls and buildings. In the 1970s, graffiti became an art style popular among many young people living in the cities of the United States.

hoppin' John: Traditional southern dish made of black-eyed peas and rice. When eaten on New Year's Day, it is said to bring good luck.

indentured servant: A person contracted to work without pay for a set period of time in exchange for food, clothing, shelter, and passage to the American colonies.

Jackson, Jesse: (1941–) African American civil rights worker and politician who has twice run for the Democratic nomination for president of the United States.

Karenga, Maulana: (1941–) African American teacher and community leader who created Kwanzaa in 1966.

kente cloth: Traditional cloth made in Ghana by sewing together long, narrow, handwoven strips of fabric.

King, Martin Luther, Jr.: (1929-1968) African American minister in the Baptist Church and a leader in the civil rights movement. Martin Luther King, Jr., was a great orator who believed in nonviolent protest to achieve social change.

Kiswahili: (KEE-swah-HEE-lee) Term used by native speakers when referring to Swahili, a Bantu language of East Africa. It is spoken primarily in Kenya, Tanzania, Uganda, and in the countries that border them. Kiswahili words are used during Kwanzaa because more than twenty million people in Africa speak it as a second language. It is also a "trade" language that people use in Africa for completing economic transactions.

kufi: (KOO-fee) Hat worn by Africans and African Americans, usually made of patterned cloth or leather.

legacy: Aspects of culture handed down by ancestors to future generations.

libation: Offering of food or drink to honor ancestors.

spirituals: Religious songs created by enslaved Africans in America and still sung in worship services.

Truth, Sojourner: (c.1797–1883) African American woman and former slave who struggled for freedom and for equal rights between blacks and whites and also between men and women.

Tubman, Harriet: (1820–1913) African American woman who escaped from slavery and returned to the South nineteen times to help three hundred other slaves to reach freedom. She was a courageous "conductor" on the Underground Railroad, a system of safe houses for escaping slaves.

Ujamaa Market: Market that is held on the fourth night of Kwanzaa. It focuses on African goods and features African-inspired entertainment.

Washington, Harold: (1922–1987) First African American mayor of Chicago.

X, Malcolm: (1925–1965) Self-taught African American who became a leader of the Black Muslims in 1952 and an advocate of black nationalism. He encouraged black people to rediscover their African heritage and culture.

Young, Whitney, Jr.: (1921–1971) Director of the Urban League during the 1960s, a group dedicated to fighting discrimination and poverty in America's cities.

INDEX

Numbers in *italics* refer to pages with photos.

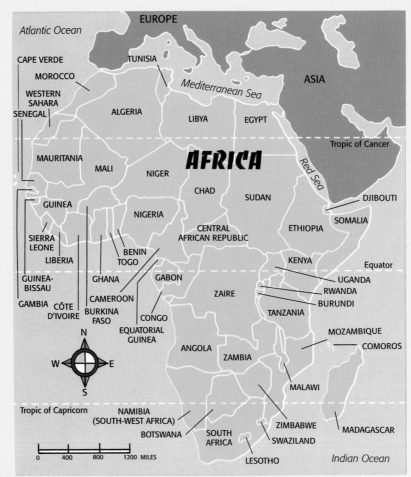